Prayers and Poems

Prayers and Poems

Monica Furlong

A note on inclusive language
The prayers reflect a time when people were striving to make the language
of worship inclusive, and to include women in liturgy and worship in many
other ways. The poems were written and published before anyone had
become aware of the need for inclusive language.

First published in Great Britain in 2004 by
Society for Promoting Christian Knowledge
Holy Trinity Church
Marylebone Road
London NW1 4DU

British Library Cataloguing-in-Publication Data
A catalogue record for this book is available from the British Library

ISBN 0-281-05668-4

10 9 8 7 6 5 4 3 2 1

Designed and typeset by Kenneth Burnley, Wirral, Cheshire
Printed in Great Britain by Ashford Colour Press

Contents

Introduction

Monica Furlong's life spanned the second half of the twentieth century, but her friendships and her writings will continue to influence people throughout the world for many years to come. Women's lives changed utterly during this period as the availability of contraceptive medicine and the possibility of creating income for themselves freed them to seek control over their own futures. Their new identity changed their relationship to men, the world and the Church in very radical ways, and challenged their own view of themselves. Monica Furlong's greatness lay in her ability to perceive and articulate this change.

I first met Monica when she was speaking at a conference of the Movement for the Ordination of Women at Clare College, Cambridge, in 1987. She shared the podium that day with Deaconess Una Kroll, who had urged her into the movement. That day the two women spoke in a way that represented very different strands of Christian spirituality. Una had been burnt by a consuming anger – her own and that of others – which flared after the rejection by the General Synod in 1976 of a proposal to further discussions towards the ordination of women to the priesthood. That Synod had witnessed her cry 'We asked for bread and you gave us stones', by which she became a heroine of the movement but also a symbol of the victimization of prophetic women in the history of the Church. Una's brave move forwards from this was a way of prayer and silence, of quenching anger by not permitting it to reign within the self or towards others. She preached therefore a sort of *via negativa*, urging women to pray, to behave politely, to move forwards carefully, not to rend apart the fabric of the Church.

Monica on the other hand was hopping mad! She preached a *via positiva* that day, encouraging us to know our emotions and not stifle them, to follow a path of self-assertiveness and self-expression as a way to enjoy the campaign and to resist being stereotyped by men or by ourselves. She encouraged rebellion, self-definition, play, even, new ways of praying, worshipping and indeed leading the Christian life! I was mesmerized.

I knew that I had not yet discovered the self that Una was encouraging us to give up, and that I was not ready to understand a prayerful life as a life of powerful protest. But I was ready to find someone with integrity who would help me see that by understanding myself, by appreciating my unruly emotions and desires as much as my more acceptable characteristics, by concentrating on enjoying life more than worrying about the disciplines and routines of the Church, I might find and express the God whom I had always loved.

Monica's speech that day, stuttered as it was, attracted and thrilled me. Here was a bright articulate woman who knew that the fear of life itself may be masked by a Christian faith that emphasizes self-denial. She urged us to be less respectful and frightened of our so-called Fathers-in-Christ who were ignoring our pleas for justice for the sake of their own convenience. She understood how women are even more prone than men to interpret the call of Christ in a masochistic fashion. What's more, she was fun! In a book Monica wrote for children called *Robin's Country* she describes 'Dummy', a tiny boy, wandering as an orphan around a fearsome wood, until he falls through a thicket of thorns into a den of friends. The friends become his gang, and health and self-esteem flow from this belonging and being together and fighting for justice. The gang has a charismatic, mischievous, risk-taking leader, Robin Hood. That day in Cambridge I found my gang, and I had found its leader.

This book of poems, with the selection of prayers, may act as a rich seam penetrating into the mine of Monica's experiences and beliefs. People wishing to explore further must read the bibliography at the end of the book. Nevertheless, here are the themes of her life: the desolation and joys of childhood; belief in God; the difficulty of developing self-confidence as a woman in Church and society; the bringing together of sexuality and spirituality; a way of faith that lives in love with the ordinary, having known both ecstasy and limitation. Monica's originality lies for me in her close attention to the opportunities to experience bliss, contentment and unity with God while leading an ordinary life. If these poems and their introduction tempt the reader to explore further those paths of bliss, contentment and unity with God, then this volume will be a fitting memorial to a friend who was my guide through the appallingly painful maze of being a woman in the Church of England in the second half of the twentieth century.

One of the themes of Monica's writings, whether biography, novel or poem, is that of the desert. Whether exploring the literal or inner desert, the image of wilderness and its necessity in her life haunted her. She knew well the scenery and its demands. The years of her childhood led, in her early twenties, not to blossoming but to desert.

In the 1940s and 1950s while Monica was growing up, England was hugely confused about what it wanted of its daughters. Were they to be educated like men? After all they had held many jobs usually performed by men in the war years. Were they to confine their sexual development to the guidelines laid down by the Church, although contraceptives were becoming available and freedom had been experienced due to shifting patterns of human relating forced by the war? Was the pinnacle of achievement for a woman to remain a white wedding in church, although church attendance itself had suffered an almighty blow in the awareness of God's inability to save us from our own inhumanity? Society's answer to these tensions was to enhance the feminine, perhaps hoping wistfully to return to an earlier supposed golden age of settled gender politics and sturdy families. Repression was preferable to confronting what the industrial revolution and two world wars had done to established patterns of faith, work and private life.

Monica found herself caught painfully in the middle of these tensions as she grew up. Different nationalities, faiths, gender expectations and frustrated hopes roared around her boisterous family life, as did the comforting experiences of evenings around the radio, and Saturday high tea. Her father, the Irish immigrant of the poem 'The immigrant' in the first section of poems called 'Jubilee', showered her with love, and bequeathed to her his indignation on behalf of women, but he grew more coldly distant as she became more able. Nor was her mother a useful person to help Monica realize her special powers and abilities, as she herself was frustrated in her marriage and ambitions. She was unhappy that Monica was quite simply not a boy-child who would deliver her from the fate of dissatisfaction with her husband; she becomes the disapproving waspish figure of the poem 'Rhymes' in this same section containing poems about Monica's childhood.

While primary school and local library fed Monica's lively mind with satisfying food, secondary school left her totally unprepared for the challenges ahead. While aware that she was intelligent, she was not groomed for university and, after a disastrous interview at Oxford, she was left to flounder and to apply for secretarial qualifications as her parents wished. By her early twenties, Monica was plump, depressed and lacking any sense of being able to achieve a profession or vocation. Adding insult to injury, the one decent post she did gain, as a telephonist and secretary with the BBC, became impossible for her owing to the effect of her stuttering on her telephone manner. While Monica had not suffered abuse as a child, she had endured that silent invisible pain of so many children – of being too grossly misunderstood to have that foundation of basic trust that permits directed energy to flourish early and easily. She is the awkward, invisible angel growing in 'Almost a real person'.

Another common theme in Monica's work is the discovery of a saviour figure, and by now Monica had discovered the first such figure in her own life. Being forced to attend Sunday school as a child bore fruit in a relationship with a friend Monica would always describe as the best and most important priest she would ever know. In her teenage years Joost de Blank gave her permission to doubt while pursuing belief and to live fully while following Christ. She had read widely in the Christian tradition so that, while finding church boring in its conservatism, she nevertheless carried into her first formative battle in the desert a longing for faith in God. In the poem 'Jubilee', which begins this book, the stage is set for a writer who will always know that the religious experience of a person will be developing in life itself often quite apart from the approval and pronouncements of the Church.

The exact location of Monica's first desert was the weed-infested, rubble-strewn ground surrounding Fleet Street, where she worked in the 1950s. The scene was built on damage, as she felt herself to be. Here she could escape the critical invasion of her thoughts by mothers, teachers, managers and colleagues. Her self-confidence at a low ebb, Monica longed for religious faith, yet felt lacking in integrity. Her intellect would not permit her to believe in God simply because she needed to! She was rescued by religious experience itself. The glory of sunlight behind heavy clouds became the doorway to an overwhelming sense of being loved, held, understood, forgiven by God and, later, to a sense of being at one with the universe, which she had not experienced since being a small child.

Later Monica was to wonder whether she was experiencing a fragmentation of her personality or whether she had fallen at last into the hands of the living God. She was never to know, but this watershed experience was to lead her later to explore far more profoundly the links between psychology and religion. From now on Monica found herself linked with all those whose experience of life contains inner desert – the mad, the bad and the mystic – those disciples following the ironic Christ in the poem 'The ironist'. This link she would pursue with sympathy and compassion, sometimes heedless to the risks involved to the self, throughout her life. I remember on one occasion, trained by now as a social worker to give myself space from the Church, and full of new knowledge about 'boundaries' and 'projection', I sat transfixed and horrified on her sofa in Ladbroke Grove as she described strange visitors coming to her home for help. I started to object, to warn, to give advice, before the realization dawned – one of those strangers was me!

If childhood has proved impossible, early adulthood has little chance of running smoothly. The experiences of the next decade provided Monica with the background material to the poems in the next section 'Reassessments'. The huge reassessment needed in Monica's own life was of her own capacity to maintain her marriage. At the age of 23 Monica, desperate to fulfil her sexual identity and to be rid of the struggle to prove herself as a woman with men, married. Her husband Bill was to be a faithful partner for many years, and was never to neglect the fathering of their children nor ignore Monica's needs in the last period of her life. Yet the pair soon began to grow apart as a couple, Monica seeking intellectual fulfilment, an exciting career beyond housework and, she would admit in later years, the Mr Right who would help her forget her own inner fears and inconsistencies. The poem 'A marital problem' succinctly expresses and disguises her own excruciating dilemma. She found herself an intellectual adventurer married to a good person who nevertheless could not fulfil her needs. What fulfilled them both was the birth and parenting of their children.

Later Monica likened birthing to writing and described them as the most important experiences of her life, filled with fear and ful-filment. At this period she began to write for the *Spectator* about religion and published *With Love to the Church* in 1964. She had seized on writing in her childhood as a way to escape into her own private but purposeful world and to integrate some of the tensions within herself. Now she began to write of her own religious asceti-cism. She gave up lending too much weight to religious disciplines like confession, realizing that human hopes, actions and motiva-tions need understanding at a far deeper level than the literal and obvious. Experience started to come first for her, before its analysis into categories of 'sound', 'pure' or 'sinful'. She raged against religious theories that sustain the suffering of others, and realized that it is only in failing religious ideals that we admit the animal within us and come to live humbly and simply in that light. Her own failing marriage helped her to criticize a Church that may use the idea of the indissolubility of marriage as a punishment for those who have simply made a mistake of immaturity. There grew in her a contempt for inhuman beliefs of all kinds within all the churches, and a love of Christ not because he shows us the way to be right but because he suffers with us the human life we live (see 'The ironist' and 'Christus').

In this period, Monica reassessed everything, impelled by the extraordinary shock of finding that though she was 'good' and 'Christian' yet she could not hold her marriage together. In the poems 'Reassessment' and 'Better not' she explored a possible fear of sex lurking behind the Christian insistence on chastity. The poem 'Pretence' questions whether apparent 'goodness' is not sometimes a veneer covering anger, rage, and violence: guilt and virtue are not easily assessable. Are we not, the poet asks, both the victim and the perpetrator of crimes against love? In 'Pietà' she unpeeled further levels of human definition, asking who is male, who is female, in Christian art and human sexual relationships. She had become one of Jesus' broken band of crooks herself.

From her mid thirties, encouraged by friendships with Harry Williams and R. D. Laing, Monica became intrigued by the dialogue between religion and psychology, translating ideas from one language to another to test their truthfulness. This led her to seek help for herself from a Jungian analyst. Monica discovered that what was hardest for her in leaving her husband was the poverty it revealed within herself, that she could be part of the cause of profound unhappiness to others. With this realization sinking in and with the approval of her mother, Monica left her marriage, deciding to defy the Church in its views of right and wrong and to carry through and support her own decision-making. Despite the awful pain of the slow rupture in her life and family, when she managed to buy her own flat and the decree absolute came through, she felt she had begun her own life: she was a woman with a room of her own.

It is the poems of this mature woman that are found in the sections 'Revelations', 'Unicorn' and 'Valley of dry bones'. In the poem 'Gamaliel' Monica permitted herself a full-throttled criticism of the Church. She wrote from the position of pain in which she found herself while married, and in which she knew the Church preferred her to stay rather than become a divorcee. She wrote, too, from her love of the priest Joost de Blank whose own self-loathing sprang from the refusal of the Church to tolerate homosexuality despite changing attitudes in Britain after the Homosexual Law Reform Act of 1967. No belief system issuing in hate, self-blame, tyranny, torture or any form of persecution is worth the candle. Gamaliel, the freestanding individual, who resists the persecution of Christians in the book of Acts, is conceived psychologically here. He was, for Monica, that mature holy person who knows that we contain tyrant and victim, hate and love within ourselves, without needing to create heroes and villains from our projections of our inner world.

Monica's Christ, depicted in the poem 'Christus', shows us a way of life we already know we want to possess. This is an important feature of Monica's theology, one that helps us as we dialogue with a world impatient with formalized religion, creeds and liturgies, yet which seeks religious experience and a spiritual basis to life. Monica did not start her life of faith by comparing herself to Christ. Instead she examined her own experience of being herself and found herself wanting. She experienced Jesus as judge not because he identifies himself as such, but because she found herself yearning to have the ability to love that he shows. In loving to the point of being able to sacrifice himself for love he becomes God for us, becomes the meaning of our human living. We need no punitive God – there is punishment enough in knowing our own damage, our own incapacity to be and to love. Moreover, salvation has nothing to do with belonging to a club, whether the club of the Church or any other sect of pure believers. That which is saving is knowing that we too live the events of Gethsemane, Calvary and Emmaus, and we find that 'God is going our way'.

It is important to emphasize here that Monica, in concentrating on the experience of God within our human nature, is not trying to reduce the mystery of God, but to confirm the true container for us of that mystery, which is not spirit or intellectual thought or church tradition or discipline but human flesh. This is expressed most finely in the poem 'Mother Julian'. Monica perceived Julian's loving memories of her own mother, the pain of her body in the tight con-finement of her cell, the burden of her loneliness as an anchorite to be the very substance into which the energy and power of the transcendent shafts like light.

Monica's own faith was not built on assent to dogma but on religious experience. Far from shunning theological debate she relished dialogue with the tradition in which she read deeply and widely. Nevertheless it was religious experience that formed her prior awareness – particularly a sense of unity with nature in childhood and a wonder at a containing unity which held her fragmented being in love in adulthood. Aware of God and of herself in relation to others, she strove to understand Christianity and the Church from this standpoint.

If the revelation of God was vital to Monica's self-understanding, so too was the discovery of sexual self-fulfilment described simply and poignantly in the section of poems called 'Unicorn'. In these love poems religious themes such as the chosen people, the Virgin and the betrayal of Christ are interwoven with the physical and emotional experiences of being in love and loving sexually, portrayed in 'My giraffe', 'Unicorn' and 'Winter'. Yet Monica's deepening psychological understanding is here too. To remain closed to love and the lover, far from being a decision made on the grounds of moral purity and strength, may represent fearing intrusion and the imagined disintegration of the self (see the poem 'Yes and no'). Sex, death and religious ecstasy come very close to each other here. There is in sexual love a letting go to our animal nature, to the boundaries of the self, to ecstatic death.

The 1970s began for Monica with the successful publishing of her first novel *The Cat's Eye* and ended with the even more successful biography of Thomas Merton. In a sense this decade begins the third phase of Monica's life, a phase that I perceive to exemplify a third strand in Monica's asceticism and a last and mature step in her walking the way of Christ. This strand consists of her ability to care for the other, to such an extent that the well-being of the whole human enterprise had come to matter more than the comfort or dignity of the self. That the shape of Monica's empathy with the other should take the form of campaigning for women within the Church of England is not surprising. That she should protest so thoroughly and successfully for their ordination, when she herself had no aspirations in that direction whatsoever, is.

Monica had seen that the prohibition against women touching the Body of Christ at the altar, and the failure of almost all men within the Church to judge this an urgent miscarriage of justice, stemmed from our misunderstanding Christianity itself and the purpose of its container, the Church. She had always been convinced that in the Church there was too great an enthusiasm for suffering in general, and far too much readiness to accept situations that perpetuate the suffering of others. She saw examples of this in the way the Church prohibited remarriage after divorce, and homo-sexual partnerships. This leaves people with no way forward to growth in human love. She saw these prohibitions as linked with a superficiality and narrowness in the Church that ignores the needs of the person before us in favour of a theory about how they should live.

The Movement for the Ordination of Women was founded in 1979. Monica attended preliminary discussions because of her friendship with Una Kroll, which had forced her to stop blocking off the pain she had suffered simply because she was a woman. Gradu-ally she realized that she sought religion to help to heal the wounds of the psyche and that this healing is impossible as long as sexuality and spirituality are not brought together but separated by religious prohibition. It was this deep rift that Monica sought to heal in her protest, and this understanding fuelled her energy and creativity. The founding of MOW sparked off a huge plethora of papers, prayers, alternative liturgies and books of feminist theology of which the prayers in this collection are prized examples. Not that this gang could always hold together, and eventually Monica's energies and gifts were channelled into the subversive St Hilda Community for which the particular prayers in this book were written. Typically Monica perceived how protest itself becomes dry, setting up an unhelpful aridity of spirit. So she formed her own 'gang' to launch a modern parable of healing – a small church for women and men where a woman would preside at the Eucharist whether licensed to do so in this country or not! Now she was outlaw indeed, kicked out of church buildings by an incensed Bishop of London playing the very same game as the Sheriff of Nottingham in her book *Robin's Country*. Monica loved it all – the defiance of the Church, the comedy, the gang. Far less palatable for her than being outlawed was the hostility and misogyny revealed in the Act of Synod that eventually accompanied the Measure permit-ting women to become priests in 1992. Her work to raise the status and self-worth of women began again immediately with the forma-tion of the Group for the Rescinding of the Act of Synod (GRAS), a group she continued to spur forward with vigour until the actual hours of her death by cancer in 2003.

In the fifth section of the book, 'Valley of dry bones', both Lover and God have gone away. In the poem 'Love is the pain . . .' the poet mourns a lost relationship. Yet she does not blame the other for lack of love, for she too must be implicated in its failure, its poverty, its impotence. It is in this honest self-examination and humble disclosure that I find Monica such a sure religious guide. Rather than berate the oppression of the Church, it is more important to ask why we seek to live within its walls, what our rage conceals. Rather than scourging ourselves over our failure to evangelize the masses or feed the developing world, it may be significant to ask when we last spoke to our family or shared a cup of fragrant tea, lovingly made, with a neighbour. Monica knew that the battles that stem from our powerlessness and emptiness must first be fought within the self (see the poem 'Reflection'). Because her own sense of inner poverty and despair led her on a psychoanalytic journey of discovery, she was able also to empathize with the seemingly irrational pain of the other in need of comfort (see 'Panic'). Eventually, as in the poem 'Nowhere', there is a turning. In utter despair we wait for a God who creates out of absolute chaos. The desert itself becomes a place of blooming and growth.

This section ends with the poem 'A slum is where somebody else lives . . .' Here Monica's beliefs about the kingdom of God, her way of life as a befriender of many, her ethical stance of concentration upon what or who is at hand are unmasked. Monica belongs where she sees Jesus belonging, not with those who wield power over others, or who supposedly want to do the other good (or more often make them suffer), but with those who know they are in need themselves, who do not offer anything.

So the collection of poems closes with the section 'God's a good man'. Monica delighted in this phrase, quoted from a yokel in Shakespeare who sensed God in the ordinary. Here there is prayer described simply, like a still pool of water. There is a turning towards old age and the first intimations of death in the poems 'Uncle Ryokan' and 'Fire in stubble'. There is awareness of the desert in 'Cantley Marsh' and 'Reclaimed land'. There is also here an extraordinary poem – 'Attraction'.

I have tried to describe Monica living a *via positiva*, as one who finds God in exploration of the rich experiences of life, in enjoyment of the fulfilment of all the human senses. Yet I have tried too to suggest that in that positive way, along it, she found her own ascetical path. The positive way itself brought loss and the need to accommodate to that loss. The way brought a challenge to concentrate on the small, the simple, the ordinary, lest the point and enjoyment of the large picture be lost. Monica asked in 'Attraction' how may we human beings who struggle to love good things, and grow through that love, let them go. She insisted on the good of the body's functions, the worth of intellectual striving, the vital importance of learning the love of particular others. It is not the Christian's task to despise these good things, she stressed! How may we, then, give them up for the sake of the other's good? How do we relinquish our love for a person who is already married, or an insistence on wealth that drives us to over-busyness or an intellectual drive that ignores the need to communicate?

We allow their importance to be gently nudged aside, Monica suggested, by the shining of God upon us, by the bearing down upon us of a being who attracts, dazzles, leads, guides. We thus allow our lives to be moulded by a greater love. Life itself offers a path of mystical experience, of union with God. Monica felt that moulding, gave way to that life, so that she was never merely journalist or wife or mother or campaigner or friend. She was a pilgrim besotted and fascinated by her journey's end, which was God. Fortunately for us she was also gifted at describing and encouraging the journey which this book of prayers and poems depicts.

Clare Herbert, Rector
St Anne's Church
Soho, London

POEMS

Jubilee

Jubilee

'George V' said my grandmother 'is a good man'.
So I got on my bicycle and rode
For the very first time,
Past Mr Maugham, who was digging his garden.
'Look at me, Mr Maugham, I can ride a bicycle!'
And the wheels swept me on
Joy, like Easter morning, a lark inside me,
Through the fragrant suburban day.
George V, who was old and ill, never knew.

The immigrant

The thin height of you
To a child,
And the Irish accent quickly concealed;
The voice of Cork is one
I shall always carry.
It used to soothe me
When I woke from dreams
And in its sound was the sea and the fields
Where you ran barefoot.
I was cradled in jokes and puns
That hid the wound of Ireland,
And the need to leave its pastures
For Westminster, where you became an altar boy,
And the dismal streets broke your childish heart.

Almost a real person

Sometimes
I am almost a real person
On good days
They don't notice
My greenish tinge
The slant of ear and eye
Or the wings folded close
To the bladed bone.

They say
'Really, dear, you're just like one of us . . .
Not like the others! . . .' and
'Some of our best friends are Martians.'
If I try hard, I pass as one of them.

Only I want to flip
Flap my great snowy wings
That could break a man's arm.
Use these strong muscles
To unfold, unfold,
The serried ranks of golden feathers
Whispering row on row
Until their narrow room is full
Of strangeness.

Rhymes

My mother said that I never should
Play with the gipsies in the wood.
How I wish now that I had
Had a go at being bad.
My shoes may shine and my hair may curl
But it's lonely being a good little girl.

One potato
Two potato
Three potato
Four
That's the way to put on
Half a stone
Or more.
Five potato
Six potato
Seven potato
Eight
The only gain I've ever
Made
Has been in weight.

Adam

When we came from the womb
How we wept
Time engulfed us
And we slept.

Wanting the moony breast
How we cried
Desolate, not
Satisfied.

Now long afterwards
We are accursed
Humbled by hunger
As at first.

Lost is our garden
Broken the cord
Cut by cherubim
With a sword.

Reassessments

A reassessment

St Monica
Is not my favourite saint.
Moral blackmail
Is not an attractive taint.
'Give up your mistress,' she said
'And your little son, Adeodatus
Or I'll cry, Augustine, I'll cry,
Mummy *will* be grieved;
                     (not to mention God)',
And she was, Augustine, she was.

Poor Augustine,
No wonder he harped so
On original sin
Gave up his delicious affair
And took to chastity in despair.

A marital problem

I often wonder about Ulysses.
Did it really take
Ten years to get home
In a smallish sea like the Mediterranean?
Or was the reason subterranean?
He had so much to do
So much to know –
And a wife who pushed a shuttle
To and fro.
Could he have got to Hades
Without Circe?
Or discovered his incurable frailty
If he had not heard the sirens sing?
Or known his strength supreme
                         on earth below
Since he could not be seduced
By Calypso?
So much he learned too
About violence and pain
And death and what a weak,
Needy, naked thing it is
To be a warrior, but glorious too.

But afterwards, at Ithaca
How did they manage?
Penelope could talk of nothing
But the price of wool
And Ulysses' lion's head
Bowed like an ox
Beneath the yoke
Of marriage.

Better not

Christians, you may remember, don't.
Solomon did, of course,
And so did many more.
The Jews had a rich erotic imagination
Which made them such a lively nation
But Christians, you may remember, don't.
At least, not often.
There were the Adamites
Of which Bosch may, or may not, have been a member
And the *illuminati*, who thought well of the body,
While the Borgias did as was their wont
But Christians, you may remember, don't.
Hindu Tantra show the heavenly pair
Shiva and Devi joined in blisses rare.
Buddhists may, whether they will or won't,
But Christians, you may remember, don't.

Pietà

She, a sturdy peasant
Knees bent, strong, unafraid
To take the dead one on her lap.
He, pale as a flower stem-broken
Weak, graceful, limp in her mighty grasp.
'My son' she says, as David did to Absalom,
And once again we weep
For the female god and his male mother
Or if you prefer it
Just the other;
It is enough to see the naked grief.

Pretence

Philosophically
Pretence is very puzzling.
See J. L. Austin*
Whose man pretending to be a hyena
Bit his neighbour on the shin
At a party.

Psychologically
It's not so puzzling
Since even sheep
Have a raging wolf inside
And every wolf has a sheep
Bleating to get out.

I am glad you told me this,
That it isn't either/or
Willy-nilly I am wolf, sheep, both
The preying and the preyed upon.
I cannot be
Neither so guilty, nor so virtuous
Neither so wedded to my dear pretence.

* *Pretending* by J. L. Austin, Philosophical Papers.

Heaven

My idea of heaven
Is after the Norwich school:
A dyke, cows in a wide landscape,
Colours cool
A lot of grass, windswept clouds,
A watercolour sky,
A canal with boat and horse going by.
For saints I wouldn't mind
Constable, Cox, Cotman,
With Palmer; Stubbs a possibility,
Or Vermeer; I don't insist
On an English eternity,
The point is, I want a northern light
Softly illumining grass, canal and stone
And beneath the lustrous turf
The solid bone.

The ironist

Jesus, what an ironist you were.
All your best stories were exaggeration
And your best heroes crooks,
To teach us how to live.
What was it that you knew
That made the cripples walk
The blind to see?
That death's the only way to get to birth,
And brokenness the only road to grace?

Revelations

Revelations of divine love

For Julian
Christ was the tender mother
Taking the little baby to the breast
Against the wounded side securely pressed.
For other saints he was a lover
But not for Julian
He was her mother.

What lost memories of her past
Lingered there? A firelit afternoon
A tranquil woman, and Julian's petal mouth
Holding the gentle flesh, until in unity
The two of them, sharing their sacrament
Arrived with God.

Mother Julian

'For Peter Damian the cell is the fiery kiln in which precious vessels for the king are made.' *Thomas Merton*, The Cell

Julian, you are transmuted
No longer subject to the cell's closeness,
Free of morning cold, and night time sadness,
The pain of fasting and the cramp of kneeling,
The grief that comes with loneliness
And the burdens others brought.
How often did you burn, burn in the kiln,
Able only to stand and tremble,
To become a vessel for the king,
Matchless, translucent, faultless.

Be with us still, who bear our cells so badly,
Measuring the space in agony,
Counting the hours and dreaming of cool meadows
Raging within the torment of the fire.
Fan us with the breath of your great love,
And like a mother touch us in the night.

King Uzziah

'In the year that King Uzziah died I saw the Lord sitting upon a throne, high and lifted up, and his train filled the temple . . . And one cried unto another, and said, Holy, holy, holy, is the Lord of hosts: the whole earth is full of his glory.' *Isaiah 6*

King Uzziah, that nobody,
Thought of nothing much
But the pain in his gut
And when the fever took him
The cool ripple of fountains
In the palace gardens.
Dying, we are not at our best.

I hope it is like that with me.
That as I turn and twist
Blind, lost, self-absorbed
On my final bed
Young men are seeing visions
Of the mighty God.

Gamaliel

Gamaliel, you were the best
Of your bunch. Why
Persecute, you said? Goodness knows,
God can look after himself. If only,
They had listened.
No rope, stone, cross, rack, stake
In your book. Men could be happy
Or naturally miserable, shy with their sweethearts,
Be there while their children grew
Quarrel with wives, get tired of work.
No guts spewed on the battlefield
No scream of pain, creak of rack,
Splinter of bone, charring of flesh,
Whimper of child,
Armies spidering out across the plain.
How did you know (they didn't and we don't)
That the devil without is the same as the devil within?

Gamaliel, you are a man of men.
I would trade the whole ragbag of saints,
The whole boiling of martyrs,
The whole twitter of angels
For one such man as you.

Christus

I

You are mankind in section; naked life
As rings spread outward in the severed tree
You know me as I do not know myself.
You are more myself than I am me.

Why did you come? It was necessity
Since evolution knows no other law.
I owe you nothing but the processes of growth
And that is simply to admit the flaw.

I did not choose my illness nor my pain.
You might as well accuse the damaged child.
What kind of God presumes to blame the sick,
Or makes us beg like dogs till reconciled?

And yet I see that you rebuke my damage.
You mock my impotent attempts to be.
Wherever I would wish to be most human
You are more myself than I am me.

II

I never met
    the Lord Jesus
Or made a 'decision'.
And if I had
Would have taken it back
Before you could say
Derision.
A commitment problem
It's called.
Also I cannot imagine
Any club
Including the Jesus club
For which I would not sooner be
Blackballed.
On the other hand
I seem to know about
Gethsemane and Calvary
And what is more
Have descended
Into hell
Once or twice.
Been resurrected
I am glad to say
And lived to live
Another day.
Jesus, it's not so much
That we are like you
As that you go
Our way.

III

In night
day
pain
joy
I find you, and I see
You in my lover,
Child,
Friend,
All who love
Me.

In beggars,
tramps,
thieves,
tarts,
I'm supposed to find
Your face.
I have not quite
Yet
Managed
Such grace.

But in sick,
sad,
old,
bereaved,
I do sometimes guess
At your
glory,
majesty,
beauty,
tenderness.

Unicorn

Unicorn

'The very fierce animal with only one horn is called Unicorn. In order to catch it, a virgin is put in a field; the animal then comes to her and is caught, because it lies down in her lap.' *Honorius of Autun*

Virgins long for unicorns to trouble their placid sitting;
If the wild unicorn is tamed
Then so, no less wild, are they.

The enamelled field full of wild flowers
Heraldically correct, is trampled by his feet;
Only thus can camomile, cowslip, lily, yield their scent.

The virgin looks sideways through doe eyes
At the royal head and its crown,
Longing for the little-death.

'Let him come and kill me!'
'Let him *not* come . . . Let him come!'
The unicorn lies down in her lap.

Winter

Nakedness hidden beneath the rug,
'O my love, I am cold, am cold!'
Runners sing over the crunching snow,
Blades hiss over the frozen river.

Chosen people

I can never quite get over
The first blush of pleasure
At being picked for the evolutionary process
Of love.
Whereas you
Knew you had been chosen
When you found the lucky sixpence
In your cake.

My giraffe

A giraffe,
Your mind leaps nimble
Over terrain. Graceful
But joky too, sharing the joke
Of your inconsequent beauty.
Bold, eager as a child
Yet suddenly shy
Moving unseen, dappled from cover
To take me by surprise
And nudge me into life.
Then suddenly huffy
Or merely thinking of something else
Off in a tangle of legs.

When you are gone the field is quiet.
I am dull, slow, clumsy,
Dowdy
From your stylish speed.

Yes and no

No
Is a blow
Hard to inflict.
Yes
Is to bless
The hearer.
All the same
No
Can redeem
And yes
Can seem in retrospect
Betrayal.

No
Is to try
To save the
I
From its intruders.
Yes
Is to fling doors wide
Ask all inside
Need to belong
(With right or wrong)
To hell with
Truth.

I tremble
For it is
The measure
Of our love,
Its boundaries,
Since yes comes easy
As the air
We breathe.
Not to refuse
Means
Lose.

Ending

I sent a letter to my love
And wrote his name in holy love and fear.
It soon returned and scrawled upon the front
It said: 'We do not know him here.'

I put my arm about his shoulders bare
And tried to see into his deep heart's core
He said: 'What have I to do with you?
I never looked upon your face before.'

I stood before the dusty window pane
And sketched the outline of my empty heart.
He said: 'I don't know what it is you say.
The time has come for you and me to part.'

An I for an I

They talked so much of love, of 'making love',
It took me years to see it was a mimic killing.
The lover ritually kills his mistress
And the kind paterfamilias his wife.
The mime announcing not an outer but an inner death.
Both the doer and the done to yielding up the ghost;
An I for an I.
Our greatest terror and our greatest joy
Come both together into ecstasy.
We long but fear to die, our immortality
Creation, secured by this lethal act,
Brutality, welded fast to total tenderness,
As the conqueror rides home on the humbled slave.
What is our joy? Not that we love like spirits
In pure, shriven, celibate state,
But that like filings caught by a magnet
Pain, fear, cruelty, are held obedient
To love's force.

Valley of dry bones

Valley of dry bones

I said my bones don't come together,
Bone to his bone.
I lie here in the empty valley
Quite alone.

'No' Thus saith the Lord God
'My cadaver is dry
No wind to breathe upon the dead
No voice to cry.

'No rain to fill the socket
That once contained an eye,
No muscle wrapped about the joint
No living I.'

Ezekiel, speak unto me
Unloose your prophet's tongue
'Alas, my child, you know quite well
That I am dumb.'

Love is the pain . . .

Love is the pain of waking
From illusion,
Of knowing our nakedness
And confusion.
To have eaten the apple
And found the weevil,
The intolerable knowledge of good and evil.
Oh! I want to say
Enough of people.
Better to go and live
Under a steeple.
Hedge love about
With prohibition,
And never learn our true condition
That we can't love.
Impotent, frigid all
We weep
Stripped of our last collusion.
Love is the pain of waking
From illusion.

Reflection

When I see my face
In mirrors unexpectedly
I am surprised at its bold strength.
The Jewish nose confidently curved
Like a sea-captain looking to the horizon
Careless of enemies.
It does not suggest
The mutinous rage that sweeps the fragile craft
(Mr Bligh ordering lashes here and there),
Its tremulous joys when west winds blow on it
Nor yet the grief, the cataclysmic grief,
Sucking the vessel to the rocks beneath.

Two visions

Fire in the house
Burning, burning that façade
With its cruel grin.
First its mouth crumpled
In shouting disintegration
And then the rest.

I saw the worm keen, keen on the bone
The mouldered flesh growing less flesh-like
Minute by minute
Until there was only the moving mass
Of maggots rising through skin
With red heads.

Panic

When I awake
Panic flutters in my breast
Like a bird
Softly bruising its wings
On walls and ceiling.
'What is it?' I ask it softly.
'Poverty or loneliness,
Or the child pretending
To strength it never had?
Where is the pain, my dove?
There is no danger here.'
The bird does not cease
Its desolate flight;
Frantic with fear
It circles
Dumbly self-torturing.
It is too blind, too lost
To find the open door.

Second birth

Behind the close canary wires
The numbing trill of panic.
I can't get out, O God, I can't get out.
In birth I struggled
(Help, of your sweet mercy
Set this captive free).
I have heard prison doors clang
In grey corridors, beaten my soft palms
On the hard walls, my screams melting
Unnoticed in the stone.
Once
Because of Victory in Europe
A crowd nudged me off my feet
And carried me
Part of a larger animal
Towards St James's Park.
That was the worst of all.
But worse is yet to come.
In death, who will deliver me
From the body of this living death?
How I shall shriek to deaf midwives,
Who, who will deliver me . . . ?
This second birth I have dreaded
All my life, moving from life no longer life
Into the day.

Nowhere

World without bearings,
World of vertigo,
Sickness, dizziness,
Lost longitude and latitude
Self lost.
'Where am I?'
Sight, hearing
Contribute only
To our confusion.
Balance has gone
Since it is not us
But the world itself
That has lost axis.
There is no poise,
Nothing,
But head in hands to crouch
Whimpering, waiting
On our spinning platform
For God to create the world.

Desert father

There
He often watched all afternoon
A rat or spider
Seeking out its own.
Or a great bird
Pronged in the orange sky
Waiting to pick and devour

Him?
It was possible.
Fears bit him
The chain, flies, hunger
Gnawed.
Thirst
Wounded him,
Lust
Scalded him,
And devils murmured
Just beyond his reach.

No sweet virgin came to him
As to the hermit at Scete.
Only at dawn and dusk
The sky was a tender green
And in spring the desert flowered.

White stars of flowers
How he would remember them
When back among the people and the trees.
He would remember
The great starry skies
From out of which
Christ leant
In dreams
To take the sobbing infant to his breast.

Master Mammon

We threw the I-Ching
      one summer morning.
Lightly we threw and lightly got reply.
The word was poverty.
It is a hard word.
I thought of Johnson and the duns
Of Blake dying in squalor
Or Rembrandt in his bankruptcy
And hoped the word that crucified my betters
Would somehow by-pass me.

And yet it has a grace
That makes wealth coarse and ludicrous.

Dust bowl

I am possessed by spirits.
Within this skin house
This delicate balance of bones
Behind the gates
Is such violence
As could ravage the countryside
Burning the crops with the flames from my mouth
Charring the tender sheep
Turning the cool green forests
And gentle pastures
Into a dust bowl, hooray,
With my horrible glance.
Trampling blissfully on villages,
Munching up the pretty virgins
Like Satan chewing Judas,
And spitting out the bones.

I would like the Holy Ghost
To make a neat slit in my front
With his fretsaw, and let the spirits out.
Leaving me all swept and garnished,
Clean and lovely.
Would seven spirits come worse than the first?
Not if he quickly sewed me up again
In double blanket-stitch.

A slum is where somebody else lives . . .

A slum is where somebody else lives,
Help is what others need.
We all want to be the priest, social worker, nurse,
The nun in the white habit giving out the soup –
To work from a position of power,
The power being
That we are not the shuffler in the queue
Holding out his bowl.

But there is only one way into the kingdom
– To be found out in our poverty.
That is why the citizens are a job lot –
Unhappily married, the feckless mother of eight,
The harlot no longer young,
The lover of little girls, the sexually untameable,
The alcoholic, the violent, and those whose drink is despair.
Show me not, Lord, your rich men
With their proud boasts of poverty and celibacy.
They are too much for me.
Hide me from those who want to help
And still have strength to do so.
Only those who get on with their lives
And think they have nothing to give
Are any use to me.
Let your bankrupts feed me.

God's a good man

God's a good man

In this good world
The sun burns on puddles,
Clouds mass in the sky above the cooling-towers,
Snow lies on slag heaps
And detergent floats on rivers limpid as silk.
In this good world
Praise bursts from our lips
Like diamonds
As jewels from the kind princess's mouth.
In this good world
Our curses turn to praise,
Perversity perverted;
Even on the rack
We're held by joy.

The mirror

The pool in the wood is round
A bright mirror standing
When you look in it you see trees
Hanging.

In shadowed water-sky
Blue trembles into grey
As the mind steadies to be still
To pray.

Uncle Ryokan

Old Ryokan asked his nephew
To do up his straw sandal.
He did not speak of sin or spending money
Or the courtesan who filled the young man's thoughts.
He said only: 'Help my shaking hand.
A man grows old.'
Frailty and love are all we need to know;
And mostly dare not.

Fire in stubble

Tongues of the Holy Ghost appear
All over the golden field.
Pillars of sepia smoke arise
Teased out by the wind like wool
Till the men half-hidden
Look like Elijah
Or like people in old photographs;
By nightfall the field is clear.

Lord, I long for your fire among my stubble.
You have had the grain, such as it poorly was.
The empty field longs for your blistering wrath.
It longs to laugh in the joy of your white-hot rage,
To crackle and fall to ash on the dark-sweet soil,
To be killed and born anew in your furious flames.

Te deum laudamus

Yes, we do, or I do.
It's not difficult.
The world's worth praising,
Its creator
By no means hard to love.
Only I find pain difficult,
Not in a niggling 'Problem of Pain' sort of way,
But because when I am in pain
He ceases to exist.
Deus absconditus
How do I praise you?

Cantley Marsh

My sort of land,
A land of brown reeds
Black mud and rough grass,
A land where livid green
Hides the sucking mouth
Of treacherous bog.
A few coverts for birds,
The creak of pheasant
Bark of fox
Stony sandy farmland beyond.
A land
Where streams wind
In interminable wastes
Of dyke and grass.
No crops or cattle there.
Too marshy to build or farm.
A lonely land
But one where you can breathe
The salty air.
Wide skies
Finding nothing but space
That fills the eyes, the lungs, the heart,
My sort of land.

Reclaimed land

Where we sit now
Was once, in Roman times
Part of the sea-bed.
Waxham and Palling
Standing as islands
In a great estuary.
Now and again the sea returns
Plunging over the dunes
To scorch the countryside.
But mostly its slow encroachments
Are defeated by vigilance.
Honour to man
Who built his great barns
And churches
On this lonely shore.
Yet in my fantasy
I long to see the salt
Come flooding back
Bathing our wounds
In hissing oblivion
Settling over our roofs.
Is this harsh?
Or a knowledge that all things have their turn?

Attraction

How shall it die
The 'I' ?
How learn to fly
A satellite
Around a bigger 'I'?
In that flight
Reflected light
Giving it glory?
Pre-Copernican
It thinks itself the centre.
Conviction that it matters
Its silly reason flatters
It is too proud to die
And cede the victory
To another 'I'.

Eppur si muove –
It likes it not
It remembers the advantages
It has bought.
The grace of reason
And the lover's fire
Opinions, fancies
And the will's desire.
The hold of memory
The clutch of fear
Possessions, talents
And the body dear.
How give up sovereignty
Renounce all these?
It would be madness
And the death of ease.

God is what is
(Shall we quarrel then?)
The sun whose influences
Govern men.
Fatally attracting

Our waywardness
Into new tracks
Of faithfulness.
Life sprouts abundant
In that summer's heat,
And mocks with birdsong
The sad 'I''s defeat.
In green high summer
Shall the soul be won,
The rhythms of the year
Begun.

PRAYERS

Prayers for various occasions

A prayer when we need love

God our father and our mother,
You have made us for yourself,
Our hearts are restless
Till they find their rest in you.
Teach us to offer ourselves to your service,
That here we may have your peace,
And in the world to come may see you face to face:
Through Jesus Christ, our Friend and Brother.

Grace

O God who gives all that is good,
May your blessing be upon our food,
Your grace and laughter shine upon our fellowship,
Your kindness be upon our tongues,
Your peace reside within us,
And your love reign in our hearts.   Amen.

A prayer when we are discouraged

O God, we bring you our failure,
Our hunger, our disappointment, our despair,
Our greed, our aloofness, our loneliness.
When we cling to others in desperation
Or turn from them in fear
Strengthen us in love.
Teach us, women and men
To use our power with care.

We turn to you, O God,
We renounce evil,
We claim your love,
We choose to be made whole.

A prayer of praise

We adore the glory and the truth that is God.
Everything within us utters praise.
Our being is formed for this purpose and no other.
All our loves and works find meaning in you.

Jesus who shows us what God is like,
Forgive us our failure to understand
But keep us in your dazzling presence.

For there we learn the nature of holiness
And partake with you in the secret of the godhead.

A prayer in time of suffering

Jesus, who was lost and found in the garden,
Never to be lost again.
Stand by us in the darkness of our crucifixions,
As the women stood by you.
Die and rise with us in the suffering of the world.
Be reborn with us,
As love and hope and faith and endurance
Outlast cruelty and death. Amen.

A prayer of offering

We hold up our smallness to your greatness,
Our fear to your love,
Our tiny act of giving to your great generosity,
Ourselves to you.

The prayer of Jesus (Lord's Prayer)

God, who cares for us,
The wonder of whose presence fills us with awe.
Let kindness, justice and love shine in our world.
Let your secrets be known here as they are in heaven.
Give us the food and the hope we need for today.
Forgive us our wrongdoing
As we forgive the wrongs done to us.
Protect us from pride and from despair
And from the fear and hate which can swallow us up.
In you is truth, meaning, glory and power,
While worlds come and go. Amen.

A prayer for courage

Those who work for change suffer resistance.

So make us strong.

Those who do new things sometimes feel afraid.

So make us brave.

Those who challenge the world as it is arouse anger.

So grant us inner peace.

Those who live joyfully are envied.

So make us generous.

Those who try to love encounter hate.

So make us steadfast in you.

A eucharistic prayer

A eucharistic prayer

President:
O God, our Father and our Mother
The God who is and was and will be
Before and beyond our little lives.
Who made all that is.
And who is known to us in our own hearts
And in the lives of others.

We come once more to trace the pattern
Of death and resurrection
That is written throughout our world.

With the saints and ancestors
We behold that mystery
And beholding it adore you.

All:
Holy, Holy, God of all power,
Heaven and earth are full of your glory.
Come and deliver us, come and deliver us, come and deliver us,
God most high.

Blessed is the One who comes in the name of our God.
Come and deliver us, come and deliver us, come and deliver us,
God most high.

President:

(Seasonal prayer)

Jesus, on the night of betrayal, took bread,
He gave thanks for it and broke it
And gave it to his friends, saying:
'Take and eat. This is my own body which
I surrender because of you.
Do the same action to remember me.'

Then, after supper, he picked up the cup of wine.
He gave thanks for that and passed it around,
Saying, 'Everyone drink of this.
This is my blood witnessing to a new understanding;
I spill it for you and for many more to cure the
Wounds of the spirit and to take away ignorance.
When you eat together, drink like this,
And remember what I say.'

We ask you, God creator, to enter this action so that our
Hearts are moved to loving, and our fear and spite fade away.
We only partly understand what we do, and we ask you to
Fill out our intention to fulfil your divine purpose,
That all who partake of the Easter feast may be
Completed in grace.

Glory to you, and may a glimpse of that glory
Be allowed to us.

President (breaking the bread):
In breaking this bread and sharing it
We share in the death of Jesus, the pain of the world,
The hope of resurrection.

All:
And by partaking we become one body.

President (pouring the wine):
In pouring this wine and sharing it
We enter into the passion of Jesus,
The blood shed in the world,
And the hope of resurrection.

All:
By drinking we become one body.

Seasonal prayers

Advent

(At the beginning of Advent)

I open this season of Advent by lighting the first of the Advent
    candles.
May it be for us a time of waiting, in peace and hope,
for the joy that our faith promises us in the new life of Jesus.

(At the lighting of the Advent candles)

Let us be a light to the world as this candle is a light to us.
Let us strive for love, justice, truth and joy.
Let us care for others as for ourselves
And for ourselves as for others.

Christmas

We stand at the turning of the year,
The time of death and birth,
Of darkness and light,
Of sadness and joy,
And we remember the baby born in a stable
Who pours glory upon our lives.
As we give presents to one another
We recognize the love present in our world,
A love that redeems the cruelty, pain and fear.

May the spirit of Jesus be born in us this Christmas and be cradled
in our hearts.
May it bring us life – the life of laughter and generosity and
kindness and joy.
May it quicken our imaginations.
May its presence drive away fear and anxiety and greed and
shame.
May it heal us and others.
May it grow in us into wisdom and love.

Epiphany

Today we share bread and wine together in memory of the birth of
    a baby,
Of the star and the journey,
Of the courage of those who seek to give themselves.
May the light of God shine upon us in our struggles and hopes,
Our griefs and disappointments.
May the journey bring us joy.
May its ending bring us our heart's desire.

We seek to be transformed,
And the bread and the wine are the symbols of that
    transformation,
Of the secret of God which burns in our hearts.
Show us how to recognize God, and recognizing, to adore.
Make us faithful to the truth of which the star reminds us.
Let not money or success or greed or desire lead us astray.

May the star which shone upon kings and wise men shine upon us
Till we are dazzled by its beauty
And ready to commit the folly of a journey,
There to surrender our tiny possessions and our timid beliefs.
Reveal to us, as we can bear it, the mystery and the joy.

Lent

We need time, space, simplicity in our lives –
Enough bareness to discern the outline of who we are and how we
    should live.
Let us use Lent as a time of peace and reflection,
In which we withdraw from getting and spending and desiring,
And remember the love which upholds us.

Lent is a time for clarity, as when the bare boughs of winter show
    us the shape of the tree in austere beauty.
Let us clear away the clutter of our lives in order to see the under-
    lying pattern.

Easter

We worship the God who entered the extreme of human suffering,
And who revealed to us the pattern –
That joy and life are the other side of pain and death.
We hold up the unspeakable suffering we see around us in the
    world
To the tragic figure on the cross,
And it is returned to us in the energy,
Hope and glory of the resurrection.
God who imitated us,
Work out the divine pattern in each of us,
That our lives may be transformed.

Pentecost

The holiness of the dove,
The cleansing fire,
The strong wind,
Work upon our souls
To make us
The people we must be,
The people of your kingdom
Able to speak in one another's tongue.

An Easter Eucharist

An Easter Eucharist

This Eucharist was written for use by the St Hilda's Community, for congregation, priest, and six or more voices. The idea was to use the dramatic power of liturgy.

President:
They have taken away the Lord, and we know not where they have laid him.

Voices:

1
The women came to the cross
To stay beside their dying friend.
The women came to the cross.

2
The women stood
Watching the pain that was unbearable.
The women stood.

3
The women held
The broken body in their arms.
The women held.

4
The women dressed
The wounded body in its bandages.
The women wept.

President:
Sir, they have taken away my Lord and I know not where they have laid him.

5
Mary.

President:
Rabboni.

1
The women saw.
The women looked upon the risen truth.
The women saw.

2
The women told.
They told the truth of Resurrection
And they were not believed.

Pause

CONFESSION

Death is
Fear, hate, envy, avarice, greed, lust, pride, destructiveness,
violence, cruelty.

Save us from death.

Life is
Love, truth, courage, laughter, giving, creativeness, tenderness,
humility, kindness.

Give us life.

Forgive us.

When we choose death instead of life.

Light us.

To life – the life of Jesus.

May God forgive us all.
May we forgive ourselves
And one another.

GLORIA

All:
We adore the glory and the truth that is God.
Everything within us utters praise.
Our being is formed for this purpose and no other.
All our loves and works find meaning in you.

Jesus, who shows us what God is like,
Forgive us our failure to understand
But keep us in your dazzling presence.

For there we learn the nature of holiness
And partake with you in the secret of the godhead.

COLLECT

Jesus, who was lost and found in the garden,
Never to be lost again.
Stand by us in the darkness of our crucifixions,
As the women stood by you.
Die and rise with us in the suffering of the world.
Be reborn with us,
As love and hope and faith and endurance
Outlast cruelty and death. Amen.

READINGS

Old Testament   Ezekiel 37.1–14
New Testament   1 Peter 1.3–9
Gospel   John 20.11–18

Instead of a sermon, four people tell briefly what Easter means to them.

HYMN

INTERCESSION

One by one, six people light a big candle. Between each request the congregation is invited to call out appropriate names.

1
I light this candle, this beam in the darkness, because it shines in the likeness of Christ.

2
I light this candle for all the dispossessed of the world, for those who are stateless, homeless, imprisoned, tortured – that they may find Jesus is with them upon their cross.

3
I light this candle for the sick and the bereaved, that in their pain and darkness they may discern hope and resurrection.

4
I light this candle for all the hungry of the world, that they may be filled.

5
I light this candle for all those who, because of class, race or sex, feel unloved and unwanted. May they find love.

6
I light this candle for this Community, St Hilda's, which seeks a new love, a new justice, a new Christian awareness which will be resurrection for many.

All:
That the light of Christ be shed abroad in the world. Alleluia.

President:
Let peace flow like a river.

The members of the congregation exchange the kiss of peace.
Baskets will be passed round for the offertory.

HYMN

OFFERTORY

President:
We hold up our smallness to your greatness,
Our fear to your love,
Our tiny act of giving to your great generosity,
Ourselves to you.

God be with you.

And with your spirit.

We turn our faces to God.

We offer our hearts.

EUCHARISTIC PRAYER

President:
O God, our Father and our Mother.
The God who is and was and will be
Before and beyond our little lives.
Who made all that is.
And who is known to us in our own hearts
And in the lives of others.

We come once more to trace the pattern
Of death and resurrection
That is written throughout our world.

With the saints and ancestors
We behold that mystery
And beholding it adore you.

All:
Holy, Holy, God of all power,
Heaven and earth are full of your glory.
Come and deliver us, come and deliver us, come and deliver us,
God most high.

Blessed is the One who comes in the name of our God.
Come and deliver us, come and deliver us, come and deliver us,
God most high.

President:
At Easter we are close to the agony of Good Friday,
To the terrible humiliation of Jesus.
Scourged and crucified,
Mocked and driven out,
As your children are hurt and humiliated still.

Yet that same agony flowered in joy.
The flower grew in the dark of the tomb
And burst apart the rock.
In taking bread and wine
Touching, breaking, pouring, drinking,
We know that we enter the holiest mystery
And that by doing so our hearts will be changed.

Jesus, on the night of betrayal, took bread,
He gave thanks for it and broke it
And gave it to his friends, saying:
'Take and eat. This is my own body which
I surrender because of you.
Do the same action to remember me.'

Then, after supper, he picked up the cup of wine.
He gave thanks for that and passed it around,
Saying, 'Everyone drink of this.
This is my blood witnessing to a new understanding;
I spill it for you and for many more to cure the
Wounds of the spirit and to take away ignorance.
When you eat together, drink like this,
And remember what I say.'

At Easter, as at every Eucharist, we recall the days of Jesus'
Passion with wonder and love.
We ask you, God creator, to enter this action so that our
Hearts are moved to loving, and our fear and spite fade away.
We only partly understand what we do, and we ask you to

Fill out our intention to fulfil your divine purpose,
That all who partake of this Easter feast may be
Completed in grace.

Glory to you, and may a glimpse of that glory
Be allowed to us.

President (breaking the bread):
In breaking this bread and sharing it
We share in the death of Jesus, the pain of the world,
The hope of resurrection.

All:
And by partaking we become one body.

President (pouring the wine):
In pouring this wine and sharing it
We enter into the passion of Jesus,
The blood shed in the world,
And the hope of resurrection.

All:
By drinking we become one body.

THE COMMUNION

During the distribution hymns will be sung.

All:
**God, who cares for us,
The wonder of whose presence fills us with awe,
Let kindness, love and justice shine in our world.
Let your secrets be known here as they are in heaven.
Give us the food and hope we need for today.
Forgive us our wrongdoing
As we forgive the wrongs done to us.
Protect us from pride and from despair
And from the fear and hate which can swallow us up.
In you is truth, meaning, glory and power,
While worlds come and go. Amen.**

President:
Let us share our joy and our gratitude.

The congregation may clap, ring bells, throw streamers . . .

HYMN

THE BLESSING

President:
The blessing of God, in all the manifestations of God, rest upon
each of our heads this night and bring us joy and love and hope.
The blessing of Jesus, who showed us what love might be, enter
each of our hearts.
The blessing of the Spirit, who gives renewed life and energy and
wisdom, delight our spirits.

Go forth into the world and keep the faith.

Amen.

Books by Monica Furlong

Biography
Genuine Fake (Alan Watts)(1986)
Merton (1980)
Puritan's Progress (John Bunyan)(1975)
Thérèse of Lisieux (1987)

Children's books
Wise Child (1987)

The Church
C of E: The State It's In (2000)
With Love to the Church (1965)

Novels
Cousins (1983)
The Cat's Eye (1976)

Poetry
God's a Good Man (1974)

Spirituality
Contemplating Now (1971)
The End of Our Exploring (1973)
Travelling In (1971)

Travel
The Flight of the Kingfisher (1996)

Women
Act of Synod – Act of Folly (1998)
Bird of Paradise (1995)
Dangerous Delight (1995)
Feminine in the Church (1984)
Mirror to the Church (1988)

Index of first lines

The Society for Promoting Christian Knowledge (SPCK) was founded in 1698. Its mission statement is:

To promote Christian knowledge by
- **Communicating the Christian faith in its rich diversity;**
- **Helping people to understand the Christian faith and to develop their personal faith; and**
- **Equipping Christians for mission and ministry.**

SPCK Worldwide serves the Church through Christian literature and communication projects in over 100 countries, and provides books for those training for ministry in many parts of the developing world. This worldwide service depends upon the generosity of others and all gifts are spent wholly on ministry programmes, without deductions.

SPCK Bookshops support the life of the Christian community by making available a full range of Christian literature and other resources, providing support for those training for ministry, and assisting bookstalls and book agents throughout the UK.

SPCK Publishing produces Christian books and resources, covering a wide range of inspirational, pastoral, practical and academic subjects. Authors are drawn from many different Christian traditions, and publications aim to meet the needs of a wide variety of readers in the UK and throughout the world.

The Society does not necessarily endorse the individual views contained in its publications, but hopes they stimulate readers to think about and further develop their Christian faith.

For further information about the Society, visit our website at *www.spck.org.uk,* or write to:
SPCK, Holy Trinity Church, Marylebone Road,
London NW1 4DU, United Kingdom.